M000087745

Dedication

This book is dedicated to the one and only Jaxon Jones. You, my son, have given your mother and I much joy. Not until your arrival did we know the true miracle of life. You've been a fighter since day one, and one day, you too will know your strength. Until then, understand that you've inspired your parents more than you know.

Phillip's Forgetful Fortune

"Too slow!" Phillip yelled as he peddled feverishly on his new bicycle.

After learning to ride all spring, Phillip decided to test his new biking skills on this sunny summer day. Jordan, Phillip's best friend, and Zoey, Phillip's younger sister, worked up a good case of the giggle sweats, as they chased Phillip around the cul-de-sac.

"Phillip, slow down, bike pro!" Zoey yelled, mocking Phillip's amateur biking skills.

"Never!" Phillip laughed as Jordan closed in for the tag.

"Got cha!" Jordan exclaimed, gasping for air after their playful, but tiring chase.

"You might be fast on that bike, but I'm fast on my feet," Jordan said.

"Speaking of fast, I need some food, like... right now!" Zoey gasped walking up.

Neither Phillip nor Jordan could disagree with food after an exhausting day of play.

"Food? That's the best thing you've said all day, Zoey." Jordan added.

"Best thing she's said all year... I guess you've both worked up an appetite getting dusted," Phillip joked.

The three worn-out amigos decided to head back to Phillip and Zoey's house, where their mother, Mrs. Floyd, was sure to have a solution for their nourishment problem.

"How'd you learn to handle your bike so quickly, Phil?" Jordan wondered. "Just last summer, we talked about learning to ride bikes and now, you're already a perfect pedal pusher."

"Honestly, I practiced every day I could - rain, snow, or shine. Momma and Zoey thought I was crazy. But look at me now!" Phillip said proudly.

"Yeah, look at you now! Still crazy!" Zoey teased.

"Hush, pea brain!" Phillip responded sharply.

"Maybe I'll get a bike for my birthday this year as well. Then we can be riding partners. ZOOM, ZOOM, SKURTT!" Jordan acted out.

"We'll be unstoppable! Only, I didn't get this bike for my birthday. I paid for it using my savings money," Phil explained.

"Savings?" Jordan asked with a confused glare. "How can you save enough to buy an entire bike!? Either you're a super-secret squirrelly saver or your parents really increased your allowance all the way up to the max," Jordan reasoned.

"Well, I did buy it with my savings but I don't have any super saving secrets, nor did my parents give me a bigger allowance." Phillip responded, "Ma and I went to the bank in December and I realized I had enough for a bike. I usually don't take money from my savings but Ma said I've been doing a great job saving and I deserved to buy something nice for myself."

"Hold on, what do you mean you realized you had enough?" Jordan was still confused. "You mean you don't know how much you have in your savings? This sounds fully fishy, my friend."

"Yes, I just realized. Ma and I only check my savings account once a year. Why would I check it more often than that? I'm too busy biking to go back and forth to the boring bank, buddy. Honestly, I forget I even have savings until Ma drags me to the bank. Plus, the other part of my allowance pays for all my goodies. The savings part just, kind of... happens."

"Saving, shmavings, graving, cravings!" Interrupted Zoey, who was less interested in Phillip's bike purchase and more focused on lunch.

"Zoey, hush or we'll start the no talking game," Phillip used one of his personal favorite threats when Zoey would get too wild.

"Ugh," Zoey conceded, "Go ahead, talk about your sad, sleepy, sorry saving stories."

"I can't disagree, Jordan, it *is* all kind of boring," Phillip said.

"I'm not sure what your definition of boring is, but in my book, cool new bikes aren't boring. Tell me your super-secret saving strategy!" Jordan begged his friend. "How do you resist looking at your savings every day? I feel like I can't even go a whole week without wondering what's in my piggy bank. It drives me nuts!"

"Well, I don't have a piggy bank. I have a savings account at the bank. Ma set it up for me. And I don't actually put money into my savings myself. Ma and dad deposit my allowance straight into my checking account and some of it automatically goes into my savings. I don't do much of anything honestly."

"Bank account? Checking? Savings? Automatically?" Jordan clearly had more questions than answers.

Jordan was an avid piggy bank saver but hadn't heard of any of the things Phillip was talking about. Jordan always thought saving was as easy as putting his leftover change in his piggy bank. And that worked when Jordan wanted an extra candy bar after school, but no way could he imagine saving enough to buy a whole bike. Jordan didn't know this yet, but he wasn't being a super saver because he thought SAVING was for the LEFTOVERS, while Phillip knew SAVING was the MAIN COURSE and SPENDING was for LEFTOVERS.

"Maybe Zoey is right. Hopefully, I can wrap my head around this after I wrap my face around a sandwich." Jordan joked.

As the group approached the Floyd household, Phillip started to reflect on his savings account. *Why didn't Jordan know anything about saving? Is Ma right to only check the bank account once a year? Why is my savings account so easy to forget and Jordan's is the opposite?*

Once they arrived at the Floyds', Phillip, Zoey and Jordan stumbled loudly into the house.

"Hey!" Mrs. Floyd yelled, "Don't come in here disturbing the peace!"

"Sorry, Ma!" Phillip and Zoey apologized in unison.

"Sorry Mrs. Floyd!" Jordan added. "Phillip was just showing us his new bike skills. You know, the new bike he claims he bought himself, with his own savings. Either he's Boo Boo, the unbelievable bear or I have a poor, pathetic piggy bank. So, which is it Mrs. Floyd? Is Phillip the saving genius he claims to be? Do you need to teach my parents to handle my savings?" Jordan asked while hastily grabbing chips from the snack bowl.

"Teach them how to do what?" Mrs. Floyd asked.

"Teach them how to give me savings," Jordan said again, "I don't think they know how."

Mrs. Floyd laughed, "I don't give Phillip savings, Jordan, he earns his allowance with chores and he saves a little of that each week."

"Right, right, but my piggy bank does not save like his bank account does. And I don't have CHECKING$ or SAVING$, or AUTOMAzzzzN$."

"Slow down, Phillip, I don't think automationzunn is even a word. Finish your chips and you three go wash your hands while I make lunch. Jordan, we'll talk about automationzunnn after..."

Jordan, Zoey and Phillip quickly scattered to the bathroom. They raced through the hall as fast as they could without alerting Mrs. Floyd.

"Hey! Simmer down in there! Miss Floyd yelled to the kids again."

"Yes, Ma!" They responded all together.

The three amigos squeezed out of the bathroom with wet hands and empty stomachs. Mrs. Floyd made her specialty, big kids' grilled cheese with apple juice and their choice of fruit or chips. Mrs. Floyd's secret was spicy peppers and only big kids can handle spicy peppers.

The PJ'Z, short for Phillip, Jordan and Zoey, wasted no time inhaling their lunch. Zoey, the most overzealous of the group, burned her mouth quite nicely as a result of her excitement.

"Ow, Ow, Ow, Ow, Ow," She cried, signaling for her apple juice.

Knowing how dramatic Zoey is, Jordan and Phillip laughed as silently as they could... Grinning, snorting, and eventually full on laughing.

"Not even your super saving secrets could save her from her own lunch," Jordan added.

"How clever, Jordan," Mrs. Floyd sharply replied, giving Jordan the mom eye. "Zoey, what have we said about waiting until your food is safe to eat?"

"I know Ma, I know," Zoey whimpered.

"Well Jordan, I think this is a good place to continue our savings conversation. It sounds like you have a case of Zoey-itis when it comes to savings."

"Zoey-Itis!?" Jordan and Phillip erupted.

"Zoey-Itis?" Zoey pouted.

"Yes, I mean, sorry Zoey, it's true in this instance. Jordan has a hard time building his savings because he reaches to enjoy it too early, just like you reached for your sandwich too early and burned your mouth. Jordan, if you delayed reaching for your savings for a while, you would have a better result, just like Zoey would've had a better result, had she delayed rushing to eat her sandwich. That's the first rule of saving Jordan, don't touch it! That's why Phillip and I only check his savings account once a year. If we don't see it, we don't think about it; we don't touch it. Easy as that. Out of sight, out of mind. And that's easy for us to say because we aren't walking past a piggy bank every day like you. Our savings account is hard to access. In fact, Phillip can't even take out money without my permission," Mrs. Floyd chuckled.

"Wow, that sounds easy, Mrs. Floyd" Jordan said. "I guess all I need now is a bank account. Then I'll watch the money roll in, CHA CHING!"

"Almost, Jordan, all you have to do is get an account and ignore the money as it rolls in... Cha, cha, cha, ching, ching ching," Mrs. Floyd danced.

Jordan went home that night and told his granny all about Phillip's forgetful fortune.

"Grammy!" Jordan yelled when he walked in the front door.

"What's the problem, Sugar?" Granny responded, concerned about Jordan's excitement.

"Grammy, Phillip has a new bike! A nice one!"

Jordan's grandmother stood confused, waiting on him to explain his excitement. "Aaand? Granny asked.

"Aaand, he got it with his own money," Jordan continued.

"Aaand," Granny waited for Jordan's point, thinking he would be asking for an early birthday gift next.

"*Aaaand* I want a bike too!" Jordan said. "Mrs. Floyd says I can save money to buy my own bicycle or whatever else I'd like. She says my porky piggy is a poor saving partner. Phillip has a super secure account where he stores his savings! I need to ditch this play piggy and get a serious savings account started... Soooo, can you sign me up Grammy? Pleasseee?"

"Well, Jordan," Granny chuckled. "It sounds like you've had quite a day today. I knew I always liked that Floyd Family.

It's great that Phillip is learning to save at such a young age. And what a pleasure that they are sharing that with you. I'm going to call Mrs. Floyd and thank her."

"Yeah, yeah, Grammy, they are great," Jordan was excited. "But what about that savings account?" He gave his grandma a big smile.

"Pushy, pushy," Grammy replied. "Well, the banks are closed at the moment, but I have some time to take you there tomorrow."

"Score!" Jordan jumped up in the air with excitement.

The next day, bright and early, Jordan and Granny headed to their closest community bank, Caption County Credit Union. Granny knew one of the bankers there and sure enough, she was greeted by name as she walked in.

"My favorite Granny with a G! How is it going, young lady?" Ben the Banker said with a smile.

"Thank you, Ben, I am here for my grandson, he would like to open a savings account."

"Is that true, young man?" Ben asked Jordan.

"Yes, sir," Jordan said, "As a matter, of fact. My poor piggy is pushing pennies and I need some real dollars."

"Wow, I wish I would've started saving this early." Ben replied, "Way to go, Jordan, let's get you all set up."

Jordan felt richer already. Ben, the Banker, wore an eye-catching, money green suit, money green socks and played Money Money Money by the OJs in his office. Jordan could tell why Granny liked Mr. Ben. He was very kind to Jordan, wasn't bothered by answering his questions, and made sure he understood all about his new super, but not so secret saving strategy.

"So, Jordan, what brings you to Caption County looking for a savings account?" Mr. Ben asked. "Not many kids your age are willing to pinch a penny away from their allowance."

Jordan told Mr. Ben all about his friend Phillip's forgetful fortune. He went on to explain that he couldn't resist pulling money from his piggy bank for candy and, hopefully, a real bank would help him save more than his pink, porky piggy.

"Well I'm hoping we can make you a saving success, sir," Ben said. "Now tell me, how much do you want to save?"

"Well, Mr. Ben, I don't know exactly, but I sure would like to have enough to buy a new bicycle one of these days."

"Oh, I see... Well, how about this? Let's go dream shopping," Mr. Ben suggested.

"Dream shopping?" Jordan was confused.

"Yes, dream shopping. Let's find the bike of your dreams, kid!" Mr. Ben shouted.

For the next 30 minutes, Ben, Jordan and Grammy with a G searched the internet for bikes, bikes and bikes until they found the perfect one for Jordan—the Dynocycle 4000. However, Jordan seemed only half excited with his choice.

"But it costs a hundred dollars," Jordan frowned, "I'll never be able to get one of those."

"Well, hold on, Jordan, not so fast," Ben interrupted him. "How much did you say you get in allowance per week?"

"Ten dollars," Jordan replied, sounding ashamed of his "measly" ten bucks a week.

"Ten bucks?" Mr. Ben exclaimed, "You're practically rich already, kid! That's more than a lot of kids around the world have."

"I know, I know, but it sure doesn't feel like it," Jordan mumbled.

"Well, let's figure this out since you don't believe good ol'Mr. Ben. How many weeks are there in a year?" Mr. Ben asked.

"52," Jordan replied.

"Good. So, if you saved two dollars every week, you could have your new bike in just one year, (52 X 2 = 104)! Now if you saved four dollars per week, you could have your new bike in just six months! Didn't you say your friend practiced riding all spring to be bike-ready in the summer?" Mr. Ben asked.

"Yeah, that's right," Jordan said.

"Well, saving four bucks a week would get you there, kid!" Ben was getting excited.

"Wow," Jordan said, "I never would've thought such a small amount, saved over some time could make a hundred bucks so quickly. Sign me up for the 6-month plan, Doc!"

Half an hour later, Jordan was strolling out of the bank with a new account number and four bucks in his new savings account. He already had it all planned out. He would let his parents transfer four dollars of his allowance into his savings each week. He would only have candy on Fridays and Saturdays, and he would only get snacks at school if they were brought from home.

"Let the game begin! VROOMMMM, MONEY, MONEY, MONEY, MONEYYYY," Jordan danced as he came out of the bank.

Jordan was able to convince his parents to auto transfer $4 of his allowance to his savings. He told them about his big bike plans and how Granny took him to meet Ben the banker for his own secret savings account.

The first week of Jordan's saving journey was pretty rough. He couldn't help but think about the snacks he would be buying if he had those four extra dollars in his pocket. Some of the kids at school even poked fun at Jordan's new saving strategy. Bart, the bully, would make sure he ate all his snacks right in front of Jordan. Francis, Bart's best friend would do the same. But this didn't bother Jordan because he knew Francis would play in a pot of poop if Bart told him to.

"Why the long face, friend?" Phillip came beside him.

"Just having a rough time taking my mind off saving," Jordan replied. "How are you so good at forgetting that you're saving?"

"I've been saving for a while now. My spending allowance is all I expect to receive, so I don't think about any other money I might have gotten if I wasn't saving." Phillip explained.

Jordan is struggling with the same thing most other kids and adults do. The unforgiving concept of time. Things don't always happen how or when we want them to, and the more you try to rush time, the longer it seems to take. Jordan struggled with his saving strategy for a few weeks. He even convinced Phillip to buy him a snack or two on a couple school days. Phillip didn't mind helping out because he understood how Jordan felt and he, very much, wanted a biking buddy. And just as Phillip thought, Jordan began to mention his snacks less and less. After a few weeks of struggle, Jordan was beginning to become accustomed to his new spending limit.

As Jordan's savings struggles improved he began to walk through the halls with the same pep in his step as before.

"How's it going, PJ?" Mr. Zudah asked, peeking out of his classroom door. "Ready for our class this afternoon?"

Mr. Zudah was Phillip and Jordan's Math teacher. PJ stood for Phillip and Jordan, of course. Mr. Zudah gave them one name because he claimed never to see them apart.

"Always ready for your lesson, Mr. Zudah," they both agreed.

"Awesome, see you this afternoon, fellas."

Mr. Zudah tutored Phillip and Jordan after school on Thursdays. Not because they were bad at math, but because they showed a great interest in it. Phillip and Jordan met after their last class of the day and walked to Mr. Zudah's classroom. Mr. Zudah's classroom was all the kids' favorite. He had math facts on the walls that all the kids talked about. He had all types of crazy activities to teach math and gave out prizes to his best students. And to Mr. Zudah, the best students weren't the "smartest" but the ones that give the most effort. For example, Mr. Zudah once asked his first period class to solve a riddle.

He told them, "Cutting a cake into 8 pieces is possible with just 3 slices, can you work out how?"

The kids pondered, half interested until Mr. Zudah pulled out 12 mini chocolate cakes from his dresser and told the class that nobody would eat until the class figured out how to cut them into 8 pieces using three slices. The kids all huddled together and started sketching practice cakes on paper and making imaginary cuts. Using teamwork and focus, the class figured out the riddle in three minutes. Mr. Zudah gladly kept his promise and devoted thirty minutes of class time to cake and educational cartoons.

"PJ, what's new?" Mr. Zudah asked.

"Not much, Mr. Z, Jordan has been saving for a new bicycle so we can be bike buddies next year," Phillip said.

"Wow, that's awesome, guys. How's that going for you, Jordan?"

"It's going okay, Mr. Z, the first couple of weeks were very hard, but it's getting better."

"Understood, Jordan, hang in there. Before you know it, you'll have your new bike and won't even notice how it happened so fast."

"That's what Phillip tells me. I'm just waiting, waiting, waiting..."

"Well," Mr. Zudah said with a thinking look on his face, "I may be able to help you fellas get to your goal faster. I change my classroom decorations with every change of the season. Fall will be here in no time and I'll need some help making the change. If you guys have a day or two, I'll pay you twenty bucks each."

"Twenty bucks each!?" Jordan whispered. "If I saved all that, it would cut a month off my saving time."

"Sounds like you fellas may be interested?" Mr. Zudah said.

"Of course, Mr Z. When do we start?"

"How about next week? We will spend half our time on math and the other half, we'll tackle these decorations."

"Awesome! We'll see you there Mr Z!"

That Friday, Jordan went home with Phillip after school. Mrs. Floyd was eager to hear how Jordan's saving journey was going.

"How's your new, not-so-piggy bank treating you, Jordan?" Mrs. Floyd called out from the kitchen.

Jordan played it cool, but he couldn't wait to tell Mrs. Floyd that he'd been sticking to the plan.

"Saving is going well, Mrs. F!" Jordan poked around the corner. "Why, what did Phil tell you?"

Jordan was afraid that Phillip told Mrs. Floyd about his beginner's struggles.

"Good," Mrs. Floyd said. "Saving can be difficult. There's always temptation in the form of things you want but don't need. Friends and family can find it difficult to understand your goals or even treat them serious at all. I'm glad you're not experiencing those things."

"Well," Jordan responded. "It was rough, passing on my favorite candies the first week. And one of our classmates, Bart, gives me a hard time about passing up on sweets."

"That's all normal, Jordan; sometimes people get jealous when you do something they can't. They attempt to hide their jealousy by making fun of your success, so don't let that bother you."

"Well, that makes me feel much better, Mrs. Floyd. Phil is always helping me when I'm feeling discouraged. I'm not sure what I'd do without him! And the best news is Mr. Zudah offered Phillip and I twenty bucks each to change the decorations in his classroom."

"Twenty bucks each!? Wow," Mrs. Floyd was pleasantly surprised. "Phillip you didn't tell me about this," She yelled into the living room.

"It just happened, Mom, I didn't have a chance to tell you," Phillip yelled back.

"Well, that's excellent, boys, what do you plan to do with your new riches?"

"I'm going to save 18 bucks and take two bucks for snacks next week," Jordan smiled mischievously.

"That's a good idea, Jordan. You are saving plenty of money by saving the 18. I'm glad you're also deciding to enjoy some of it. That's important as well."

"Phillip, what do you plan to do with your fortune?"

"I think I'm going to use it to buy Zoey a birthday present." Phillip said.

"Good idea! I'm sure your sister will really appreciate that."

"Hmmm she better," Phillip pondered. "Now Phil, you know part of having is giving. Zoey might get a nice birthday present but you'll also receive the satisfaction knowing that you used your money to bring joy into someone else's life. Some people never experience that feeling because they are so selfish with their money. They think if they spend some on a good cause, it may never come back. In reality, it's quite the opposite. The more you help others, the easier it is to get your money back."

"I know, Ma, I know. I just don't want to see her snotty grin when she gets my cool gift, that's actually cooler than her."

"Be nice to your sister, Phil. And you boys get ready for dinner." Mrs. Floyd said.

After dinner, Jordan had a great idea.

"Mrs. Floyd, I've been thinking, what if we asked all our teachers to change their decorations? We could charge $20 each."

"That's an excellent idea, Jordan! Make sure you approach every teacher with kindness and thank them even if they decline."

"Of course!" Jordan and Phillip exclaimed and went to work on their pitch for the rest of the night.

When they returned to school the next week, PJ wrote down all the teachers that decorate their doors. They made a schedule of when they would present their idea to each of them.

By the time they finished their schedule, it was Thursday already. Both Jordan and Phillip were very excited about their first job. They discussed their idea with Mr. Zudah while they tore down and rehung his posters.

"That's an excellent idea, fellas. When you finish my classroom and I'll be sure to let all your future customers know what a great job you did. Even better, they'll be able to see the finished product when they walk past my classroom!"

"Thanks so much, Mr. Z," The boys replied. "We'll make sure your classroom has a fall, festive, phenomenal feeling."

Phillip and Jordan finished half of the decorations on Thursday and completed everything the very next Thursday. Even the half-finished decorations caught the eyes of many teachers. They got 10 new clients from just a half-finished design. Once they were completely finished, they had 20 of the 30 teachers that decorate their rooms ask them to do it for them. According to their schedule, they would need to stay after school every day for the next two weeks and complete two rooms per day.

Phillip and Jordan met at Jordan's house to discuss their plan for completing the huge project. Jordan and Granny also visited the bank that morning to deposit $18 of Jordan's profit from Mr. Zudah. At the bank, Jordan noticed that his savings were already at $50 ($32 saved over 8 weeks and $18 for Mr. Zudah's payment).

Wow, I'm halfway there already, Jordan thought. *This is an extraordinary, excellent turn of events.*

Jordan couldn't wait to tell his friend about his progress.

"Phil, I'm already halfway there! Me and Granny went to the bank and I have $50 already!"

"See, my friend, I told you. It flies by."

Jordan and Phillip executed their plan perfectly over the next two weeks. They were both so worn out when they finished; they forgot they just made $200 each! They were so excited about doing a good job in each classroom. In fact, they did such a good job that they were featured in the school newspaper as "Students of the Quarter" and received

a special trophy for their creativity.

Jordan and Granny visited Mr. Ben at the bank to deposit his earnings.

"Hot dang, young man, what kind of savings have you been doing?" Mr. Ben was surprised to see Jordan request $200 to deposit.

"Well, Mr. Ben, I've been saving for 10 weeks and I've saved $40 already! However, me and my friend, Phillip started a business at school that paid us the rest of the money."

"Wow, Jordan, that's so impressive," Mr. Ben said. "Not only how much money you made but also how much you were able to save. I bet you'll be getting that new bike sooner than later!"

"Oh yes, Mr. Ben, I'll be getting my bike this weekend! I'm looking forward to learning to ride all winter and showing my skills off next spring."

Phillip, Jordan, and Granny with a G purchased the Dynocycle 3000 Jordan had been waiting for that weekend. Jordan came over every weekend possible, so Phillip could teach him how to ride.

Phillip and Jordan continued helping their clients change decorations as the seasons changed. They even got other kids at the school to help them balance their new workload. After word spread about their booming bike-inspired business, they taught their friends at other schools how to build their own room decoration business.

"What a crazy year it's been, Phillip. All because you showed me your super-secret savings strategy." Jordan said.

Phillip laughed, "It's not so secret anymore, my sensational saving super friend. But what you'll want to keep a secret is how I'm going to dust your dooopy dyno cycle."

"Oh is that right?" Jordan smirked back. "Don't doubt the dyno dude. Today, the student conquers the teacher."

"Ready, set, go!"

Made in the USA
Middletown, DE
15 February 2021